S0-AJH-707

Deliciously Raw

Easy Recipes for the Omni Blender

by Carmella Soleil

Also by Carmella Soleil

The Best of The Sunny Raw Kitchen
The Best of Raw Freedom Community
Delightfully Raw

www.thesunnyrawkitchen.blogspot.com
www.rawfreedomcommunity.info/forum

DELICIOUSLY RAW: EASY RECIPES FOR THE OMNI BLENDER © Copyright 2010 by Carmella Soleil. All rights reserved. This book may not be reproduced in whole or in part by any process without written permission from the copyright holder except in the case of short quotations for the purpose of reviews.

First edition
Published by Carmella Soleil in collaboration with Omniblender.com, LLC
3507 E Bay Court
Eagle Mountain, UT 84005
USA
Phone 801-623-3225
lifestyle@123vita.com

www.3blenders.com

Cover and Book Design by Carmella Soleil
Front and back cover photos of Carmella by Don Lacey. Food photos on back cover, as well as photos on pages 18, 22, 32, 38, 57 and 66 by Jaime Lynn Hagel. All other photographs by Carmella Soleil.

ISBN 978-0-9867858-3-2

DISCLAIMER
The techniques and advice described in this book represent the opinion of the author based on her experience. None of the statements contained in this book have been approved by the FDA. The author expressly disclaims any responsibility for any liability, loss or risks, personal or otherwise, which is incurred as a result of using any of the techniques, recipes or recommendations suggested herein. If in any doubt or requiring medical advice, please contact the appropriate health professional.

Contents

Foreword

*A*s a chef, I'm always on the lookout for new gadgets and appliances to work with in my raw kitchen. During a recent stay at the Foxes near Salt Lake City we were introduced to the Omniblend V blender; a powerful 3 HP blender that costs significantly less than comparable machines.

Don and I run our blender a minimum of 3 times daily. We use it for making smoothies, dressings, sauces, soups, spreads, puddings, pie and cake fillings, ice creams... and I'm probably forgetting something! After buying regular inexpensive blenders (we gave them such a work out that they had to be replaced at least once a year!) we began to save our pennies in order to purchase a high-speed blender. Not only was it a great deal more powerful but it also gave such a silky smooth texture to everything we prepared. It was like entering a whole new world of possibilities! How I wish that we had known about the OMNI back then; we would have certainly found it easier financially to take that (for many of us HUGE) step from the 'cheapo' blenders to a high quality one!

Needless to say I was excited to put the OMNI to the test, and was in fact so impressed with it that I accepted Thomas' offer to write a recipe book especially designed for it. We've been using the OMNI for all of our food prep in the last 3 weeks or so and are positively surprised by its consistent performance.

The recipes contained in this book are all simple, quick to prepare and utterly delicious! The fact that they are also raw vegan and therefore in our opinion super healthy really is just a bonus! Our intention is to provide you with recipes that are 'good for you' and yet are so tasty that you'll feel inspired to use your OMNI blender regularly. It is my sincere hope that wherever you are along your health journey that you will have fun experimenting with them and even perhaps creating some blended recipe concoctions of your own.

Here's to your health!

Carmella ☀

Carmella Soleil
St George, Utah
January 2011

In a Raw Nutshell

*A*s I like to say, I'm a 'hands-on kinda gal'. I find myself a lot more at ease when talking practical food prep stuff rather than venturing into intellectual aspects of raw diet and nutrition. Frankly, I continue to choose to eat raw foods primarily because of how good they make me feel. As part of my own healing journey, I've managed to gradually become more sensitive to my physical sensations. This has allowed me to pay closer attention to how I feel and give my health the importance that it deserves.

*T*hat being said, I can completely understand that some people need to know the 'whys' and 'hows' of something before they feel moved to explore it. In this section, I will be giving a brief overview of my take on the health benefits of eating food in its natural, raw state. For those of you that want it, I figure there are lots of passionate folks out there that can walk you through all the juicy scientific details better than I ever could!

So Why Raw?

Very simply put, in the process of cooking our food it has been shown that the following changes take place:

- the live enzymes it contains are killed,
- amino acids and essential fatty acids are destroyed, and
- a large percentage of the vitamins and minerals are altered in such a way that our body cannot assimilate and utilize them properly.

On the other hand, when we consume food that has not been exposed to heat above approximately 118ºF, enzymes stay alive and can then fulfill their critical functions. See, enzymes are what our bodies need to break food down. If those that are naturally present in food are dead, then the burden falls on our pancreas to produce them. In other words, by eating raw and living foods, we're giving our body a huge break! The energy that would normally go towards digesting food can then be allocated elsewhere; to tasks such as eliminating toxins, strengthening the immune system, rejuvenating cells and fighting disease.

The pH of Food

Another reason why we feel eating raw contributes to better health has to do with the pH of food.

One way to describe our bodies is that they are super complex bio-electric engines. What generate electrical power in our bodies are very finely balanced bio chemical processes. Our blood stream is probably one of the most important systems that rely directly on this delicate balance. Now let's take a closer look at how this relates to pH and why it plays such a decisive role in our health.

pH is a scale that measures how acidic or alkaline a substance is. The scale ranges from 1 to 14, with 1 being very acid, 7 neutral and 14 very alkaline. Research has shown that the ideal pH is around 7.35. Our bodies will go to incredible lengths in order to maintain this level, because if our blood pH were to vary much in either direction, it would so dramatically change the chemistry that we would lose electrical power - much like a vehicle that loses its battery power - and we would die.

Here's how it works...

Each of our cells has a nucleus and a surrounding liquid within a membrane. The nucleus is acidic and the liquid is alkaline. This polarity is required for the proper electric charge transfer. When our blood pH is too acidic, it acidifies the cell liquid and the charge transfer potential is thereby reduced. Also, many studies have shown that disease needs an acidic environment within the body in order to manifest.

It has been found that our body's pH is determined by what we eat and drink. However it isn't quite as straightforward as it seems. For instance, we may think of a lemon as being very acidic, but at the ash level (in other words, when it is digested) it is actually alkaline. Unfortunately, many of the foods that make up what is known as the Standard American Diet (or SAD) create an acidic ash. These include coffee, black tea, pop, alcohol, virtually all animal products, most grains and legumes, as well as processed foods. On the other hand, most fruits and vegetables are alkaline and so are nuts and seeds, once they have been soaked or germinated.

My Health Journey

*A*lrighty! *slapping her hands together* Now let's move on to less theoretical matters and tell you a little about my story, shall we?

*F*or as long as I can remember, I've always loved food. My mother told me that I used to walk into the neighbors' house and help myself to my favorite cookies in their cupboards! lol But my relationship with food has been "tough love" at best! Ironically, I have a very delicate digestive system. In fact, I was conceived while my dad was dying of stomach cancer. Coincidence you think? Nah, not in my book! In addition to my difficulties digesting certain foods, particularly meat, I also had food allergies; a fact I only came to realize at the end of my 20s. There was a time when I was afraid of eating altogether because of the almost inevitable stomach pains that were sure to come along.

*A*good way to describe the person I was in what I now think of as 'my previous life' would be to say that I was almost completely out of touch with my body, and therefore also my feelings. A close and very intuitive friend of mine, having picked up a slight change in my mood, once asked me how I felt. And you know what? I was unable to answer that! I had no idea how I truly felt inside. It later became apparent that the only way I managed to cope with living in a stressful, toxic city environment was to cut myself off from feeling the many physical and mental discomforts that were plaguing me.

*E*ventually, in 1995, inspired by my sister's own dabbling into the vegetarian diet, and no longer being able to 'stomach' the way eating meat, poultry and fish made me feel, both physically and psychologically, I became a vegetarian. Even though my new diet did help in some ways, I was still far from thriving.

*B*y 1999 I was in the worst shape I'd ever been in my life. I had quite a few extra pounds and was suffering from a number of health issues. I was extremely irritable and depressed, had chronic vicious mood swings, insomnia, migraine headaches, low energy, constipation, and my digestive problems hadn't let up. (Pfhew!) During the last winter I spent in Quebec, I only got the flu 5 times! lol I would barely recover from one virus before I was hit with another. Enough already!

When a naturopath offered to do a reading of my condition with some new and complex computer device, I thought: "What the heck! What do I have to lose?" Even though I was relieved, at some level, to find out what was going on inside my body, the news was far from comforting. It was determined that all of my organs and meridians were totally out of balance (surprise, surprise!), except for my heart (thankfully!) According to the reading, I was also suffering from candida, and had allergies to foods such as corn, gluten and dairy. And, to top it all off, my immune system was completely shot to pieces. It's amazing that I was still standing! The naturopath basically told me that I might as well be throwing all the good organic foods I was buying straight down the toilet, as my system was too weak to even absorb the nutrients.

As you can imagine, I walked away feeling pretty shaken up, not having a clue as to what to do with this newly found knowledge. Where does one even start, when everything seems to be so out of whack? As it turned out, I had to wait a few more months before I began to find the answers.

The Leap into the Unknown

My first realization was that my general state of unhealth was only the tip of the iceberg. Deep down, I was unhappy and unfulfilled; my life was going in circles and now I knew it. I was 29 and in my Saturn Return - a period of internal upheaval, during which one reconsiders what has been working so far and, most importantly, what hasn't. And so, I decided to walk away from everything that made up my world at the time, in order to jump into the Unknown. As a result, in the summer of 2000, I left Quebec in the hopes of getting a fresh start on the other side of Canada. I didn't have a clue where I'd live or what I'd do in British Columbia. All I knew for certain was that I was long overdue for a serious change. Within a very short time though, three major things happened to solve my quandary.

1. Landing on Don's doorstep. Quite literally! I'd been in BC for a grand total of 3 days when in Victoria, on Vancouver Island, I came upon an ad for a room to rent. As I was due to leave the next morning, I made arrangements to check it out on the way to the ferry. After giving me the tour, Don told me: "I think you'll be happy here!" Boy, was he ever right! We were destined to become platonic life partners and he was destined to be instrumental in my new journey of self-discovery.

2. The 14 day Master Cleanser. I decided my body was in dire need of a fast after all the abuse I'd put it through over the years. Doing the cleanse had a powerful impact; it helped me see with greater clarity what bad shape my body was in and how I needed to start taking better care of it. Amongst other things, it prompted me to start doing 'The Five Tibetans'; a surprisingly simple yet powerful and energizing set of exercises, which I still do almost daily.

3. Vipassana Meditation. It also became clear that my mind needed a fast even more badly than my body did! I was fortunate to hear about a type of meditation called Vipassana; a Pali word meaning 'to observe reality as it is'. Even though this technique was re-discovered by Buddha, it is nevertheless non-sectarian, which helps explain its tremendous appeal to people all over the world, regardless of religious background. On the Vipassana website, it is described as "a way of self-transformation through self-observation. It focuses on the deep interconnection between mind and body, which can be experienced directly by disciplined attention to the physical sensations that form the life of the body, and that continuously interconnect and condition the life of the mind." What I experienced and learned during those 10 days of silent meditation shook me to the core. It prompted me to focus inside in order to free myself from my fears and cravings. In fact, I still use the Vipassana technique everyday, as I find it incredibly simple and effective.

I was on a roll! And so this all led to my embarking on a journey so profound that it was to completely change my vision of the world.

What About Raw?

Embracing a mostly raw vegan lifestyle came along as part of the inner transformation I was undergoing. Don, for his part, had been experimenting with diet ever since he became a vegetarian in 1980. Shortly thereafter, he ate nothing but raw fruits and nuts for 7 months, which he still considers to be the time when he felt the greatest in his entire life. It's only later, in 1995, that he was first introduced to living foods through friends who ran a small raw café out of their house. In 2001, both of us gradually started including more and more raw foods into our diets, while at the same time paying close attention to the issue of control. (More on this in the next section.)

If we refused to get caught in ideals and control how we should eat, then how did we manage to change our diet? This is difficult to explain, as it isn't a linear thing. One way to describe it would be to say that it began with our unbending intent to lead more fulfilling, healthier lives. The improvement in our diets - which has been slow and gradual over the years - has only been a side effect of our process of personal growth. That's not to say that our diets have been 'perfect' (if there is such a thing!) or that we haven't made so called 'mistakes'; but the overall trend has been ever improving. Our main approach consists of honoring where we're at, and this connects to the quantum physics understanding that objectively observing 'What Is' (or facing facts) will transform.

When you don't recognize who's staring back at you in the mirror!

I'm fascinated by 'Before and After Raw' pictures. Don reminds me, though, that everything is a reflection, and therefore it's my own incredible transformation that I see represented in them. When I visited my family in the summer of 2005 (for the first time in nearly 6 years), they hardly recognized me! It's difficult for me not to think of who I used to be 'back then' as a different person altogether. Hang on a minute; let's see if I can dig out some old photos somewhere…

In the top three photos I was 20 years old and at my heaviest, 140 pounds. I had just returned from an important but challenging backpacking trip to Europe where I consumed copious amounts of bread, cheese and beer. lol

The bottom left was taken about 6 months after I became vegetarian in 1996. My weight then hovered around 125. In the right photo I was vegan and my weight had settled at around 120. A few months later I was heading west and embarking on my raw journey.

The top left photo on page 10 was taken in 2005, after 4 ½ years on a mostly raw food diet. Sorry for the large gap but I couldn't find any good photos for that period. My weight basically remained the same for the entire time; about 100 pounds in the summertime and 105 in the winter. The next photos were shot after my going 100% raw in the summer of 2006. And yes, I somehow managed to lose a few more pounds. The last photo was taken this summer back on high raw. I'll get into a little more detail in the next section, but in the winter of 2009 we began to reintroduce some cooked foods into our diet. Since the beginning of this year, I've been experiencing my body changing and getting curves I never had before (my weight now hovers around 106). At first I thought that the stress from our traveling was the main culprit, but now I'm convinced that it has to do with something shifting at a hormonal level as I'm approaching 40.

Before

Winter 1991   Summer 1991   Summer 1991

Summer 1996   Winter 2000

After

Summer 2005

Summer 2005

Summer 2006

Spring 2007

Summer 2008

Summer 2010

I Feel So Dif-fe-rent (Or The Ongoing Transformation...)

As incredible as it may seem, most of the physical problems I experienced prior to eating more raw foods have disappeared. The constant lethargy that used to overcome me has been mostly replaced by a vitality I never knew was even possible. Other significant changes that I've noticed include a dramatic improvement in both my hair and skin, much better digestion and elimination, no more bloating and a stronger immune system (I've only had a cold once in 10 years!)

In 2003 I was diagnosed with SAD (Seasonal Affective Disorder), aka 'Winter Depression', a condition I undoubtedly had for many years. I only managed to shake it off after we transitioned to a fully raw lifestyle in 2006. I'm always a little hesitant to give credit for what I might be experiencing, be it at a physical, psychological or energetic level, to any one particular cause. (I mean, how can you REALLY know for sure what has brought changes?) However, making the jump to a fully raw diet does seem to have directly contributed to my on-going transformation.

Here are some of the changes I experienced during that time:

* I had no cravings for cooked food (and I mean zero, none, ziltch!)

* I didn't feel 'internally' cold as I did in my 2 previous 'raw winters'

* My sleep was deeper and more restful

* I was more stable both mentally and emotionally. The pronounced mood swings I used to go through mellowed out dramatically. (Just ask Don, he'll corroborate! lol) I felt more balanced, not getting so caught in the extremes of feeling like "Everything is hunky-dory!" or "That's it... I'm doomed!"

* I had virtually no depressive, pessimistic thoughts

* I experienced very little conscious fear or anxiety, to speak of

* I didn't feel the usual lethargy in the wintertime. (In the past, there were days when I could hardly get out of bed...)

At this point, I'm still allergic to certain foods and occasionally get an upset stomach. I also experience carpal tunnel syndrome, which is probably genetic related. One thing that has tremendously helped is that I've learned better how to stay in touch with my body and how I'm feeling at any given time.

Don's story is quite different than mine. For one thing, he has been working on improving his diet for a lot longer than I have. He has also been blessed with one of those 'cast iron digestive systems', which changes the picture considerably. His weak spot is his kidneys. When he was still in the Canadian army (yep, you've read right! Talk about past lives!) he suffered a massive internal infection from which he never fully recovered. As a result, his kidneys would hurt whenever he consumed any kind of cooked oil. Switching to a mostly raw diet immediately solved the issue. While he has always had a strong constitution, Don's overall health has nevertheless improved. He certainly doesn't look or feel like the 62 years old that he is and he continues to enjoy what seems like boundless energy.

Our Approach To Changing Diet

We feel that changing what foods we eat is not an end in itself and can't be about an ulterior motive such as losing weight. It must be part of a much bigger process of improving oneself and one's quality of life. We have found that true personal transformation starts from the inside out, not the other way around. In my case, I didn't consciously decide to become 'vegetarian' or 'vegan', it just gradually happened; meat was the first to go, then poultry and fish, and a few months later dairy. At a certain point, embracing a mostly raw lifestyle felt like the natural next step. It's the inner work that I've done that has given me the energy (and interest) to start taking better care of myself. And in turn, the food I eat gives me more energy to focus on my inner work. lol

A major turning point for me was when I was able to truly see that the use of control, whether in general or in regards to diet, doesn't support health or growth. Yes, perhaps on the surface control allowed me to make 'healthier' choices in terms of what I ate, but at what price? I would obsess about food all day (and night!), have bouts of binging, and then later be tormented with guilt and shame that I 'knew better' but couldn't 'do better'. How healthy was that?

It is our experience that control is actually using force (willpower) against 'What Is', and as such it is a distortion of the natural energetics of things. This process will give temporary results at best, and in the long run because of its inherent repression and conflict, bring its unwelcome opposites: excess and obsession. At best, it just temporarily covers over 'bad habits' and causes us to waste, in the internal conflict, the very energy that we need in order to permanently kick them.

We think this is one of the main reasons why any form of imposed dieting can only work in the short term. Sooner or later, as we say in French, "le naturel revient au galop." ("Nature comes galloping back!") While working on this book, I received an email from a woman that was very apropos. She shared that although she noticed a dramatic improvement in her physical health following the 80-10-10 diet, she also experienced a profound dissatisfaction. She said that she felt unsatiated, bored, like she'd been missing out, very nostalgic for her old foods, and even craving ones she hadn't eaten in over a decade, such as meat. She also felt "somewhat fanatical and obsessive" about what she will eat or just ate. Sadly, I wasn't surprised at all to hear her story; it was very similar to my own.

There seems to be an extremely fine line between acting from a place of true 'knowing' (actually 'seeing' that something isn't 'good for us') or from control. As far as I can tell, the difference lies in how much energy one has; while the former comes from awareness, the latter comes from ideals and concepts of what 'should be done'. Another way to put it is that one is based on feeling, the other on thought. Don pointed out to me that there is a difference between getting an internal "Yes!" about eating certain foods versus a hidden craving that finally gets a chance to pop to the surface. When I asked him what he meant, he went on to explain, "See, if I'm not controlling or addicted, I may, for example, feel an urge to eat salmon one day and then not again for months or even years. On the other hand, if it's a craving, eating it once will trigger a certain compulsion to have it over and over again, like a reformed alcoholic can't have just one drink."

I once heard that you can tell if a diet is really working for you by whether you have cravings. We feel that this is true. Since discovering the benefits of a raw lifestyle more than 10 years ago, at one point it felt completely right for us to eat 100% raw, but that lasted for only 2 ½ years. By that I mean that during that time it seemed natural and effortless and wasn't accompanied by cravings for any cooked foods. I remember thinking that it felt much like when I gave up meat; it was so darn easy, which I know is because it was in perfect harmony with where I was at. During our recent travels we met an old seasoned raw foodist at a potluck who had worked alongside Gabriel Cousens at Tree of Life. He said he felt that it's virtually impossible to sustain a fully raw diet unless one lives on a mountaintop. It gave us a good chuckle, as that has been our exact experience; when we ate 100% raw we lived at a retreat center that was located on a mountain! lol In hindsight, we see that one of the main reasons we were able to stay raw had to do with the unique circumstances of the time; we were under minimal stress, had a lot of free time and energy to prepare food, and had almost no exposure to cooked foods.

What to do then? How does one go about bringing positive changes in one's life without exercising control?

We have found that an effective approach is to honor where we are at and fully embrace it, moment to moment. If we can simply observe objectively whatever's happening, without judgment or condemnation, then we can begin exploring the facts: "Why am I eating things that I know aren't good for me?" We feel that because it's what's happening, it follows that we are always doing whatever we have the energy to do at any given time. It really helps us avoid the traps of blame or guilt, which are even more energetically debilitating. We have learned that if we take the risk and simply continue to observe our undesirable habits (whether it's food, alcohol, coffee, etc,) without attempting to control, they eventually start to change; a fact that has now been proven by quantum physics.

The journey towards health and wholeness is surely a never-ending one. We still go through phases where we don't eat as optimally as we theoretically could, but we're able to face it and move on. Because it's what's now going on doesn't mean it will always be that way. Whenever that happens to me, I do my best to maintain my awareness throughout the experience. This allows me to integrate ever more deeply into my being the actual knowledge of how certain foods make me feel.

Nine Helpful Tips for Successfully Transitioning to Raw Foods

LOOK AT IT FROM THE PERSPECTIVE OF INCLUDING MORE RAW FOODS IN YOUR DIET, NOT CEASING TO EAT COOKED. The more raw you eat, the less room there'll naturally be for cooked foods; it's simple cause and effect!

LEARN THE 'LAY OF THE LAND'. As for any cuisine, raw food prep is like a world of its own. I would recommend building a raw reference library by collecting recipes and food preparation tips. If, like me, your budget is a little tight, you'll find a wealth of information on the Internet, especially on forums such as Raw Freedom Community. You may also want to consider checking out your local library. If it doesn't carry the raw books you're interested in, it probably has an inter-library loan service that can order them for you.

FIND A DOZEN OR SO RAW RECIPES THAT YOU REALLY ENJOY. The fact is that we mostly tend to gravitate towards the same staple dishes. When you don't feel like whipping up new recipes and being creative, you'll have some tried and true no-brainers and won't be confined to salad or carrot sticks, or worse, be compelled to quickly grab some crappy cooked junk food.

SIMPLE IS BEST. One of the beauties of raw foods is that you can eat as simply or extravagantly as you want; from munching on a crisp apple or a juicy tomato to dining on lasagna, dehydrated pizza or other gourmet dishes. If you're new to raw, I would suggest starting with easy recipes and gradually working your way up to more involved and complex ones. As for many things, there is a steep learning curve and you don't want to run out of steam. It's amazing how many tasty dishes can be prepared in one or two steps with the help of a blender or food processor!

IT'S NOT ABOUT EATING 100% RAW. You will experience benefits from any live foods you include in your diet! If you were to enjoy a fruit or green smoothie and a raw soup every day, that alone would enable you to consume a considerable amount of raw fruits and vegetables.

DON'T MAKE RAW INTO A RELIGION. I know how thrilling it can be to start noticing our bodies transform and our health improve on raw foods. You may feel so darn good that you can't help yourself wanting to 'preach about raw' whenever you get the chance. While your friends and family will undoubtedly be happy for you, it doesn't mean that it's the next step on their journey. The most powerful motivator will always be your example. As you continue to progress on your healing journey, it will automatically show. Whoever is ready to take steps on their own health path will come to you.

STAY FLUID AND KEEP AN OPEN MIND. Remember that Life is constantly changing! If you look closely, you'll notice that it consists of phases within phases within phases. Because something feels absolutely right for us now doesn't mean it will always remain so. After eating 100% raw for over 2 years, our circumstances changed and we started reintroducing some simple alkaline cooked foods into our diet, such as quinoa, baked squash and potatoes. Again, this wasn't a conscious decision on our part; it somehow felt like the right thing to do. Because of my highly sensitive digestive system, this was a very painful process for me, as my body no longer tolerated cooked. However I am so very grateful that I hung in there, as being open and able to eat some cooked foods once in a while has proved to be so helpful during this new phase of being on the road. It has simplified things a lot when we find ourselves camping or staying with non-raw hosts.

TAKE IT AS AN EXPERIMENT. It can get pretty confusing as to 'what is best for us' (whether for life in general or when it comes to diet), as we're constantly being bombarded with contradictory information from right, left and center. It's so easy to move away from our personal experience and get caught into someone else's reality. Here's a couple of rules of thumb that we have learned and found to be helpful along the way in dealing with this difficult issue.

1- Don't Believe Anything Anybody Else Says (Including Me!)
No matter how respected or knowledgeable someone is (or seem to be) about something, we suggest you take it with a grain of salt and experience for yourself what really works for you (or doesn't!) Until that happens, it is going to be nothing but intellectual concepts.

2- It's All An Experiment Anyway!
Don and I try to approach everything in our lives not as something static and fixated, but rather as an experiment; a fun, everlastingly new and fascinating adventure, its outcomes remaining unknown. Whatever happens, we feel it's all about learning more about ourselves and how to be in the world.

AND LASTLY... BE GENTLE AND PATIENT WITH YOURSELF! Don't forget that the way we behave and the food we eat is very deeply ingrained in our beings. Most of us have badly abused ourselves for decades so we can't expect things to change overnight. It takes a lot of dedicated care and tremendous amounts of energy to begin to turn the tables around and relearn how to nourish ourselves from a place of true knowing rather than mere idealizing.

Ingredients

This is not intended as an extensive list of all the ingredients used in raw food preparation, but rather a glimpse at those most frequently called for in this book. As a general rule, for maximum health benefits, whenever possible I recommend that you choose organic, unprocessed, and raw or unpasteurized ingredients.

CACAO – Cacao refers to the unadulterated and unprocessed cacao fruit, which grows on a jungle tree in Amazonia. Unlike the more common cocoa (notice the spelling difference!), raw cacao hasn't been subjected to high heat or chemicals and has no added sugar or milk. Also known as the 'Food of the Gods', cacao contains high amounts of vitamins, minerals, various nutrients and 'happy brain chemicals', such as theobromine, phenylethylamine (or PEA) and tryptophan. It is also considered one of the world's most powerful antioxidants.

In raw food prep, it is mostly used in the form of beans, nibs, powder and butter (which is firm at room temperature and gives a wonderful subtle flavor to desserts!)

CAROB POWDER – Carob has a sweet taste similar to that of cacao, but with a lower fat and calorie content. It can be used in almost any recipe as a substitute for, or in combination with, cacao powder.

CHIA SEEDS – Chia seeds originally came from South America and were a major staple for the Aztecs for centuries. Dubbed "Nature's forgotten superfood", they are a phenomenal source of omega-3 fatty acids, dietary fiber, antioxidants, complete protein, iron, calcium, and magnesium. When soaked in water, chia seeds swell and form a gel. We make a wonderful pudding by soaking chia seeds in nut milk for at least 20 minutes and adding some sweetener, vanilla and cinnamon. We also use them as thickener/binder in smoothies, dressings, soups, crackers and even burgers.

COCONUT OIL – Coconut oil is the highest known source of saturated fats, most of which are medium-chain fatty acids that can be quickly and efficiently metabolized by the body and transformed into energy. It contains zero cholesterol and actually helps the body break down accumulated fats. After breast milk, it is the second highest source of lauric acid; the most important essential fatty acid in building and maintaining the body's immune system.

Coconut oil is firm at room temperature, which makes it ideal in raw dessert making. There was a time when coconut oil and coconut butter referred to the same product, but that is no longer the case. Coconut butter, such as the one produced by Artisana, is a combination of virgin coconut oil and creamed coconut meat.

DRIED FRUITS – Some of the most commonly used include apricots, cherries, cranberries, raisins and dates. In this book, I call for both 'soft dates' and 'Medjhools'. Please note that the former refers to smaller varieties, such as 'Barhee', 'Halawy' and 'Khadrawy' dates.

EXTRACTS – Look for high quality pure extracts at your local health food store, such as almond, orange, hazelnut, peppermint and vanilla.

PSYLLIUM – Psyllium seed husks come from the seed stalk of the common plantain. Psyllium is sometimes used in recipes in order to thicken mixtures, as it becomes mucilaginous when wet. It must be used in moderation, however, as it tends to lend a gelatinous texture.

MISO – Miso is a traditional Japanese thick paste produced by fermenting rice, barley and/or soybeans. As a general rule, I prefer light miso because of its milder flavor. It isn't technically raw as the grains are first cooked, but new enzymes develop during the fermentation process.

NUTRITIONAL YEAST – Not to be confused with brewer's yeast, nutritional yeast is an inactive yeast commonly popular with vegans for the cheesy flavor it lends to dishes. It's not raw.

NUTS AND SEEDS – Nuts and seeds are used a great deal in raw food preparation to make spreads, crackers, burgers, sauces, cheezes and desserts.

OILS – Whenever possible use high-quality, organic, cold-pressed oils. Good oil can truly make all the difference! I use cold pressed olive oil in most of my recipes and occasionally raw sesame oil.

PROBIOTICS – Probiotics are beneficial bacterial cultures often used in order to speed up the fermentation process while making sauerkraut or cultured nut cheezes. Look for probiotics in the refrigerator of your health food store's supplement section.

SALT – Salt is one of those controversial topics in health circles. It has been associated with a number of health conditions, such as water retention, high blood pressure and heart disease. If possible, try to keep your salt consumption to a minimum and use only natural unrefined salts, such as Celtic Sea Salt, Himalayan Salt or Real Salt.

SEA VEGETABLES – The most commonly used sea vegetables are arame, dulse, kelp, nori sheets and wakame. We love to add them to our soup bowls instead of salt, as they are rich in traced minerals.

SOY LECITHIN – Lecithin is derived from soybeans. It is often called for in raw dessert making as it acts as an emulsifier when combined with oil. Look for lecithin (preferably non-GMO), in granules or powdered form, at your local health food store. If purchasing granules, make sure to grind them up to a fine powder in the Omni blender or coffee grinder before adding to your dessert recipes. It isn't raw.

Soy lecithin is also available in liquid form but I find it less convenient, as it has a stronger flavor and is dark in color.

There is a raw alternative available made from sunflower seeds, but it comes in liquid form only.

SUPERFOODS – It seems that new superfoods keep popping up on the market all the time. Some used in this book include gogi berries, lucuma, maca and mesquite powders.

SWEETENERS – Recipes that require sweeteners mostly call for dried fruits, raw honey, raw agave nectar or maple syrup.

> **Agave** is another very controversial topic among the health conscious due to its high fructose content. Two types of plants are used to make agave nectar: Agave Tequilana (Blue Agave) and Agave Salmiana (White Agave). Blue Agave is processed by first removing the root or bulb of the plant which is then ground down. Water is run through it in order to pull the fibrous inulin out of the ground bulb. This fiber water is then boiled at high temperatures to break the fructans into fructose and glucose. In other words, there is no such thing as 'raw blue agave'. Agave Salmiana, or White Agave, is processed very differently. When the plant is 7-8 years old, the flower that grows at its center is cut off, creating a hole or pool of liquid known as 'Aguamiel' in the center of the plant. This liquid is left to ferment, turning it into an alcoholic drink: tequila. To obtain White Agave nectar, the water contained in the aguamiel is removed by evaporation – a process that can be done at low temperatures. White agave nectar is particularly convenient to work with as it incorporates easily and is almost flavorless.

> **Honey** – Since it is produced by bees, honey is not considered vegan, however it has been increasingly used in the raw community to replace agave nectar. Look for raw honey; the concentrated nectar of flowers that is unheated, pure, unpasteurized and unprocessed. Honey is not as versatile as agave because of its thick consistency and strong flavor.

> **Maple syrup** is not raw, but provides a rich and voluptuous flavor, particularly in combination with cacao.

> **New low glycemic sweeteners** are now available such as Xylitol (made from birch), Erythritol (made from organic sugar cane juice) and Lakanto. I, however, have personally never worked with them.

TAMARI – Tamari is a type of soy sauce that can be made with little or no wheat. As I am gluten intolerant, I like to use the organic wheat-free tamari.

THAI YOUNG COCONUTS – A true wonder of Nature! Not only are young coconuts delectable, but they are also super nutritious! Young coconut water is one of the purest forms of water available on the planet. It is very high in electrolytes and is a blood purifier. It is said to be identical to human blood plasma, so much so that it was transfused in place of blood during the Pearl Harbor crisis. The soft coconut flesh makes wonderfully creamy mixtures. Thai young coconuts are white in color and can be found at Asian markets, health food stores and some large grocery stores.

Vanilla Beans and Powder – Some raw recipes call for the seeds that are obtained by slicing the bean in two and delicately scraping them off the shell. For my part, I prefer to use vanilla beans in the form of 'Liquid Vanilla' – an awesome trick I learned from Café Gratitude. To make Liquid Vanilla, roughly chop 3 vanilla beans and blend them with 1 cup water in a high-power blender. The resulting mixture can be used in place of vanilla extract and will keep for one month or so refrigerated in an airtight container. For texture purposes, I like to use vanilla powder in recipes that don't have a water content, such as chocolate candy.

Equipment

The recipes in this book have been carefully chosen for their ease of preparation. While the vast majority can be made solely with the use of a high power blender such as the Omniblend V, I have chosen to include a few recipes that require other pieces of equipment to give you a sense of the wider range of possibilities. The following is a list of the specialty appliances/tools called for in *Deliciously Raw*. You can find a more detailed discussion of how to best equip a raw kitchen on my blog, The Sunny Raw Kitchen.

High Power Blender – The appliance that gets the single most usage in a raw kitchen! All the recipes in this book have been especially tailored for the Omniblend V blender sold by 3blenders.com

Dehydrator – A dehydrator allows one to 'cook' food at very low temperatures so that the enzymes remain alive during the process. It opens up a lot of possibilities, such as making crackers, breads, pizza crusts, cookies and nut burgers. The favorite in the raw community are the 5 or 9 tray models manufactured by Excalibur.

Food Processor – Another 'must have' in a raw kitchen! A food processor is useful for chopping veggies in a snap and working with low water content mixtures like spreads, crackers, cookies, crusts and breads. We particularly recommend the Cuisinart and Kitchen Aid brands.

Ice Cream Maker – For whipping up delicious homemade raw vegan ice creams! We strongly suggest investing in the Cuisinart models.

Nut Milk Bag – For separating the pulp from the liquid while making nut milk. Paint straining bags from a paint or hardware store, or even panty hose also work beautifully and are a lot cheaper than the specialty ones!

Spiral Slicer – A little gadget that will allow you to make beautiful vegetable pasta in no time at all! By far the best and easiest of use in our opinion is the vertical Benriner Cook Help. Alternatively you could use a simple vegetable peeler or a mandoline in order to create thin long pasta like strips.

Super Chocolate Shake

Smoothies & Shakes

Smoothies and shakes are super quick to throw together and a wonderful way to consume a lot of fruits. Enjoy them for breakfast, lunch, snacks or even dessert!

Apricot Blueberry Ambrosia

Surely this must be what Gods and Goddesses indulge in on Mount Olympus!

Serves 2 or 3

2 bananas
2 cups apricots
1 cup blueberries
1 orange, peeled and seeded
2 cups water
Juice of ½ lemon

Process all ingredients in the OMNI blender using the 60 second cycle, or until smooth and creamy.

If necessary, adjust sweetness by adding raw agave nectar or honey and blending again briefly.

Pina Colada Smoothie

A delicious smoothie with a taste of the tropics.

Serves 2-3

2 bananas
1 small orange, peeled and seeded
2 cups fresh pineapple
3 tablespoons dried coconut
1 cup water
½ cup ice
Sweetener of choice, as needed

Place the dried coconut along with the water in the container of the OMNI blender and let sit for 15 minutes.

Add the rest of the ingredients and process using the 60 second cycle, or until smooth and creamy.

If necessary, adjust sweetness by adding raw agave nectar or honey and blending again briefly.

Anything Goes Green Smoothie

I've nicknamed Don 'The Smoothie Man', as he's the one who's usually in charge of whipping them up. Here is one of the basic recipes that he often makes.

Serves 2-3

¼ medium avocado
1 or 2 bananas (fresh or frozen)
1 cup of fruits of choice (fresh or frozen)
1 or 2 cups fresh greens, such as spinach, swiss chard, lettuce and/or kale*
Juice of 2 or 3 oranges (or 1 to 2 small whole oranges, peeled and seeded)
1 lemon, juiced
1 to 1 ½ cups of water

*If using greens with a tough stem, you may want to de-stem them first to make your beverage easier to blend and more palatable.

Process all ingredients in the OMNI blender using the 90 second cycle, or until the greens are completely broken down. Add more or less water, to taste.

Sunny Raw Tip: We buy lots of fruits while they're in season and freeze them. That way we get to enjoy a variety of fruits in the wintertime, when the choices are pretty bleak.

Chia Fruit Smoothie

Chia seeds are bursting with goodness! They are full of vitamins, minerals, fiber and antioxidants. We like to add them to our daily smoothies for extra nutrition and thickness.

Serves 2

2 bananas
2 cups fresh or frozen fruit of choice, such as berries, peaches, pineapple or mango
2 cups juice or water
2 tablespoons chia seeds

Process all ingredients in the OMNI blender using the 60 second cycle, or until smooth and creamy.

If necessary, adjust sweetness by adding raw agave nectar or honey and blending again briefly.

Nut Milks

Nut based milks are such a wonderful replacement for dairy! They are very simple to make at home, and the best part is that they are fresh, raw, and don't contain any added sugar or preservatives! The most common is undoubtedly almond, but you can also whip up delicious milks using other nuts such as Brazils, cashews, hazelnuts, macadamias or pecans. The basic technique remains the same: blend (soaked) nuts with water until completely dissolved, strain and enjoy!

Basic Nut Milk
We prefer to make a neutral milk that can later be used in both sweet and savory recipes. For a sweet milk, simply add a date or two and perhaps some vanilla extract.

1 cup nuts, soaked overnight*
3 to 5 cups water (depending on how creamy and thick you like your milk)

* Brazil nuts, Hazelnuts and macadamia nuts don't contain enzyme inhibitors, therefore there is no need to soak them.

1. Process in the OMNI blender using the 90 second cycle, or until nuts are completely broken down (about one minute or so.)

2. Strain the mixture through a nut milk bag or fine mesh.

3. Store the milk in an airtight container in the refrigerator where it will keep for 3 to 5 days.

Note: Save the left-over pulp in a Ziploc bag in the freezer in order to make all sorts of yummy recipes, such as crackers, cookies or cakes.

Nut Milk in a Pinch
Blend 2 tablespoons of raw nut butter with 2 cups water. No need to strain.

Coconut Milk
Place 1 cup dried coconut and 3 cups water in the OMNI blender. Let sit for 10 minutes or so to allow the coconut to soften. Process using the 60 second cycle, or until smooth and creamy. No need to strain.

Coconut Cream
Place 1 cup young coconut meat and 1 ½ cups filtered water in the OMNI blender. Process using the 60 second cycle, or until smooth and creamy. No need to strain.

Mango Spinach Green Smoothie

Who would have thought that blending fruits and leafy green vegetables could make such a palatable and energizing brew!?! A veritable nutritional powerhouse! Green smoothies have been a daily affair for us ever since we heard about the Boutenko family's story. We mostly use whatever fruits are in season and the following is just an example of one of the many delicious concoctions that we whip up.

Serves 2

2 bananas
1 mango, fresh or frozen
1 orange
1-2 cups fresh spinach, according to taste
2 tablespoons gogi berries (optional)
Juice of ½ lemon or lime
Water, until desired consistency is reached
Sweetener of choice, as needed

Process all ingredients in the OMNI blender using the 90 second cycle, or until the greens are completely broken down.

If necessary, adjust sweetness by adding raw agave nectar or honey and blending again briefly.

DELICIOUSLY RAW: EASY RECIPES FOR THE OMNI BLENDER

Super Chocolate Shake

This shake uses superfoods and is yummily addictive. It will leave you fueled up and crying for more!

Serves 2

2 cups almond milk (page 27)
1 frozen banana
1 Medjhool date
1 tablespoon cacao powder or 1 ½ tablespoons cacao nibs
2 teaspoons carob powder
2 teaspoons lucuma
1 teaspoon maca
½ teaspoon pure vanilla extract or liquid vanilla
Dash nutmeg
Pinch salt

Process all ingredients in the OMNI blender using the 60 second cycle, or until smooth and creamy.

Depending on the ripeness of your banana, you may need to add a touch of raw agave nectar or raw honey for sweetness.

Winter Green Smoothie

A simple smoothie using some basic ingredients that can be easily found during the wintertime, when the fruit shelves at looking bare.

Serves 2-3

2 bananas
2 small oranges, peeled and seeded
1 apple, peeled if non organic
1-2 cups fresh greens of choice, such as spinach, swiss chard, lettuce and/or kale*
Juice of 1 lemon or lime
1 tablespoon chia seeds (optional)
Water, until desired consistency is reached
Sweetener of choice, as needed

*If using greens with a tough stem, you may want to de-stem them first to make your beverage easier to blend and more palatable.

Process all ingredients in the OMNI blender using the 90 second cycle, or until the greens are completely broken down. Add more or less water, to taste.

Carobanana Shake

When we served this drink to a non-raw friend of ours, she smacked her lips in satisfaction and declared: "Mmmm... Very nice! I'd definitely say "yes" to that again!"

Serves 2

2 medium frozen bananas
2 cups almond milk (page 27)
2 Medjhools (or 3- 4 small dates, soaked)
2 tablespoons carob powder
2 teaspoons pure vanilla extract or liquid vanilla
Pinch nutmeg
Pinch cinnamon
Pinch salt

Process all ingredients in the OMNI blender using the 60 second cycle, or until smooth and creamy.

Strawberry Banana Shake

Another scrumptious and satisfying drink using almond milk as a base.

Serves 2

2 cups almond milk (page 27)
2 medium frozen bananas
2 cups strawberries, fresh or frozen
¼ cup soft dates
2 teaspoons pure vanilla extract or liquid vanilla
3 tablespoons lucuma (optional)
½ ice cubes

Process all ingredients in the OMNI blender using the 60 second cycle, or until smooth and creamy.

If necessary, adjust sweetness by adding raw agave nectar or honey and blending again briefly.

Soups

We think of raw soups as savory smoothies. They are a fabulous way to consume lots of fresh veggies in a flash! Don and I have been enjoying them daily since 2001. There was a time when we'd throw nearly everything but the kitchen sink into our soup concoctions… all at once! What we've learned, however, is that simple is actually best. We throw in 2 or 3 vegetables, a little miso, and add seasonings/herbs of our choice, along with some water. And the secret to making delicious, creamy soups lies in using avocado or perhaps some nuts or nut milk .

Having said that, we don't really care much for cold soups, especially when our bodies crave warmth in the wintertime. At first, we used to gently heat up our soups on the stove at medium, stirring constantly until lukewarm. However, since becoming nomads, we've taken to using hot water instead. Provided that there's enough bulk, the coolness of the vegetables combined with the heat of the water brings the mixture to the perfect lukewarm temperature. To make sure that we don't overheat those precious enzymes, we like to start with a small amount of hot water, blend and test for temperature. We then add more cold or hot water, depending on what's needed, until the desired consistency is reached. This technique requires a bit of getting used to, but once you get the hang of it, is so much quicker!

Also, we usually prefer to add dried seaweed to our soup bowls at the end, rather than using salt – a great way to consume trace minerals.

So Like Campbell's Tomato Soup

Remember Campbell's Cream of Tomato Soup? I virtually grew up on the stuff! This next recipe reminds me of it, only much better in every way, of course!

Serves 2

2 cups roughly chopped tomatoes
2 cups roughly chopped red bell peppers
½ cup almonds or cashews, soaked for 8 hours
¼ medium avocado
Juice of ½ large lime
1 teaspoon light miso
Salt to taste
Fresh or dried basil (optional)
Water, until the desired consistency is reached
Raw honey or agave nectar, if needed

Process all ingredients in the OMNI blender using the 60 second cycle, or until smooth and creamy.

Add more hot or cold water, as needed, until the desired consistency is reached.

If the soup tastes too acidic, add a squirt of raw honey or agave nectar and blend again.

Popeye Gone Raw Spinach Soup

As I often like to joke, I love spinach so much that I may very well be Popeye reincarnated! One of my favorite ways to enjoy this nutritious and iron packed green is also one of the simplest: in soups. I've made several variations of the following using different herbs, and it always hits the spot. Try it; you might become a convert too!

Serves 2 to 3

½ medium avocado
4 cups spinach, packed
2 cups roughly chopped cucumber
1 cup roughly chopped zucchini
1 cup roughly chopped tomatoes
1 celery stalk, chopped
1 green onion, chopped
1 garlic clove
1 tablespoon lemon juice
¼ cup (or I handful) parsley
¼ cup (or I handful) cilantro
1 teaspoon light miso
Salt to taste
2 cups water, or until the desired consistency is reached

Process all ingredients in the OMNI blender using the 90 second cycle, or until the greens are completely broken down.

Chia Garden Soup

This past summer we've been successfully experimenting with using chia seeds in soup to replace part of the oil and avocado.

Serves 2-3

2 cups roughly chopped zucchini
1 ½ cups roughly chopped cucumber
½ cup roughly chopped red or yellow bell pepper
¼ cup roughly chopped carrot
¼ cup parsley
1 celery stalk, roughly chopped
1 tablespoon cold pressed olive oil
1 tablespoon chia seeds
1 garlic clove
2 teaspoons dried thyme
1 teaspoon light miso
½ teaspoon dried sage
Salt, to taste
Water, until the desired consistency is reached

Process all ingredients in the OMNI blender using the 60 second cycle, or until smooth and creamy.

Add more hot or cold water, as needed, until the desired consistency is reached.

Tomato & Herb Soup

Ahhh! Big juicy tomatoes and fresh basil; some tastes of summer! Here is a simple soup with a lovely, delicate flavor. The key is to use ripe, sweet tomatoes and fresh herbs.

Serves 2

½ small avocado
2 cups roughly chopped tomatoes
1 cup zucchini, peeled
1 garlic clove
1 green onion, roughly chopped
2 tablespoons fresh basil (packed)
1 tablespoon fresh oregano (packed)
1 tablespoon cold pressed olive oil
1 teaspoon light miso
1 ½ cups water
Salt, to taste

Process all ingredients except 1 tablespoon of basil in the OMNI blender using the 60 second cycle, or until smooth and creamy.

Add the left-over basil and pulse briefly. (You want to keep some of the herbs intact.)

Note: If your tomatoes aren't quite sweet enough, add a teaspoon or so of raw agave nectar or honey to the soup so as to take some of the acidity away.

Don's Pilgrim's Soup

Don has a real knack for coming up with excellent soup concoctions. In this recipe he uses Jerusalem artichoke, which gives the soup a slightly sweet and earthy taste. Yum!

Serves 2 to 4

½ medium avocado
3 or 4 celery stalks, roughly chopped
2 green onions, roughly chopped
1 small (or 1 cup) zucchini, roughly chopped
1 small tomato, roughly chopped
1 medium Jerusalem artichoke, roughly chopped
Handful of parsley
Handful of cilantro
1 tablespoon light miso
1 tablespoon raw tahini
2 cups water or until the desired consistency is reached

Process all ingredients in the OMNI blender using the 60 second cycle, or until smooth.

Add more hot or cold water, as needed, until the desired consistency is reached.

Note: No need to peel the artichoke before using it; simply scrub it well under running water and cut off any dark spots.

Cream of Leek

The following emerged from one of my all time favorite soups, Jennifer Cornbleet's Cream of Zucchini. One day when I was missing some of the ingredients, I went with what I had on hand. The result reminded me of the cooked Cream of Leek I so loved as a child.

Serves 2

½ medium avocado
1 ½ cups roughly chopped zucchini
¼ cup fresh parsley
1 stalk celery, roughly chopped
1-inch piece of leek
1 ½ teaspoons lemon juice
1 teaspoon light miso
¼ teaspoon salt or to taste
Dash cayenne pepper
1 ½ cups water or until the desired consistency is reached

Process all ingredients in the OMNI blender using the 60 second cycle, or until smooth and creamy.

Cheezy Spinach Almond Soup

As is often the case, some of the best recipes sort of happen unexpectedly. Last summer I had almonds soaking with the intention of making my So Like Campbell's Tomato Soup on page 58, only to realize that there was no red bell pepper to be found in the house! I ended up creating this instead, which has been a huge hit with a lot of people, including us.

Serves 2-3

2 cups packed spinach

1 ¼ cups roughly chopped tomatoes
½ cup almonds, soaked for 8 hours
¼ cup fresh parsley, packed
¼ cup fresh dill, packed
¼ medium avocado
1 tablespoon nutritional yeast
½ teaspoon salt (or 1 teaspoon light miso)
1 garlic clove
Water, until the desired consistency is reached

Process all ingredients in the OMNI blender using the 90 second cycle, or until smooth and creamy.

Add more hot or cold water, as needed, until the desired consistency is reached.

Creamy Sweet Pea Soup

A house favorite that is simple, tasty and oh-so-filling!

Serves 2

½ medium avocado
1 ½ cups sweet peas (thawed if frozen)
1 cup roughly chopped cucumber
1 cup roughly chopped celery
⅛ cup fresh dill
⅛ cup fresh parsley
1 ½ teaspoons lemon juice
½ teaspoon light miso
1 clove of garlic
½ green onion, roughly chopped
1 ½ - 2 cups water, until the desired consistency is reached
Salt, to taste

¼ cup sweet peas for garnish

Process all ingredients except ¼ cup peas for garnish in the OMNI blender using the 60 second cycle, or until smooth and creamy.

Add more hot or cold water, as needed, until the desired consistency is reached.

Divide remaining peas between 2 bowls. Pour soup on top and serve.

Green Cucumber Soup

This is a staple for us in the summer when there is such an abundance of cucumbers! One of the great things about raw food prep is that it's very forgiving. Feel free to play around with the amount of avocado, lettuce, celery and parsley; it will almost certainly turn out delicious!

Serves 2

½ medium avocado
2 cups lettuce, packed
1 ½ cups roughly chopped cucumber
¼ cup parsley
2 celery stalks, roughly chopped
1 green onion, roughly chopped
1 garlic clove
2 teaspoons lemon juice
1 teaspoon light miso
Salt, to taste
Water, until the desired consistency is reached

¼ cup freshly chopped dill

Process all ingredients except fresh dill in the OMNI blender using the 60 second cycle, or until smooth.

Add more hot or cold water, as needed, until the desired consistency is reached.

Add dill and process briefly only to incorporate.

Cream of Celery

This soup reminds me of the cooked version my mom used to make. So creamy and comforting!

Serves 2-3

2 cups almond milk (recipe on page 27)
2 cups roughly chopped celery
1 cup roughly chopped zucchini
⅓ cup parsley
½ medium avocado
1 green onion, roughly chopped
1 teaspoon light miso
Salt, to taste

Process all ingredients in the OMNI blender using the 60 second cycle, or until smooth and creamy.

For a warm soup, heat soup gently on the stove while stirring constantly.

Dressings

*A*lmost as important as the salad ingredients themselves is what you dress them up with. A little trick I read somewhere (and one that often comes in handy) is to experiment and find a few different dressings that you really like. That way, when you feel like enjoying a salad, you don't have to search hi and lo for something suitable.

*Y*ou may also want to consider investing in a salad spinner (if you don't already have one); a cheap and useful kitchen tool that will dramatically improve your success in making wonderful salads.

Carmella's House Dressing

This dressing has quickly become a regular favorite. Whenever I make it, I like to make lots, as it keeps really well and is always good to have on hand.

Yields 3 cups

½ medium avocado
½ cup cold pressed olive oil
¾ cup water
⅛ cup apple cider vinegar
¼ cup lemon juice
2 or 3 garlic cloves
2 tablespoons raw tahini
2 tablespoons tamari or Nama Shoyu
e nectar or honey
aste

41

n the OMNI blender using the 60 second cycle, or until smooth and

Hemp Avocado Dressing

A slightly different take on my House Dressing, mostly using hemp seeds instead of tahini.

¾ - 1 cup water
½ medium avocado
¼ cup cold pressed olive oil
¼ cup tamari or Nama Shoyu
¼ cup lemon juice
¼ cup hemp seeds
1 tablespoon raw honey or agave nectar
1 teaspoon apple cider vinegar
2 large garlic cloves
Dash cayenne
Salt, to taste

Process all ingredients in the OMNI blender using the 60 second cycle, or until smooth and creamy.

Ranch Dressing

An excellent dairy free rendition of a popular favorite!

Yields 1 ½ cups

¾ cup cashews, soaked
½ cup water
2 tablespoons cold pressed olive oil
2 tablespoons apple cider vinegar
2 tablespoons lemon juice
1 tablespoon raw honey or agave nectar
2 teaspoons onion powder
1 teaspoon dill
1 teaspoon salt
½ teaspoon garlic powder
1 garlic clove
More water, until the desired consistency is reached

Process all ingredients in the OMNI blender using the 60 second cycle, or until smooth and creamy.

Chia Mustard Dressing

This is yet another great way to use chia seeds!

¾ cup water
¼ cup cold pressed olive oil
2 tablespoons chia seeds
2 tablespoons apple cider vinegar
2 tablespoons lemon juice
1 tablespoon raw honey or agave nectar
2 garlic cloves
2 teaspoons dried mustard
1 teaspoon salt (or to taste)
1 teaspoon dried dill

Process all ingredients in the OMNI blender using the 60 second cycle, or until smooth and creamy.

You may need to scrape down the sides for those elusive little chia seed 'stickies'.

Dill-icious Dressing

A must try for all dill lovers!

Makes 3 cups

½ medium avocado
¾ cup water (or until the desired consistency is reached)
½ cup olive oil
⅛ cup apple cider vinegar
¼ cup lemon juice
2 or 3 garlic cloves
2 tablespoons raw tahini
1 tablespoon miso (or 2 tablespoons tamari)
1 teaspoon salt, or to taste
¼ cup fresh dill

Process all ingredients except dill in the OMNI blender using the 60 second cycle, or until smooth and creamy.

Add dill and pulse briefly to incorporate. Alternatively, you could finely chop the dill and add it by hand.

Curried Dressing

This dressing was meant for a kale salad recipe I played with, but it is so good that I thought it deserved to be shared on its own.

¼ cup cold pressed olive oil
¼ cup lemon juice
2 tablespoons raw tahini
2 tablespoons apple cider vinegar
2 tablespoons tamari
2 teaspoons curry powder
1 tablespoon sweetener
1 teaspoon salt, or to taste
3 garlic cloves
Dash cayenne
Water, as needed

Process all ingredients except dill in the OMNI blender using the 60 second cycle, or until smooth and creamy.

If necessary, add water until desired consistency is reached.

French Dressing

A dressing with personality, sure to jazz up the most boring salad!

½ cup roughly chopped tomato
¼ medium avocado
½ cup lemon or lime juice
¼ cup cold pressed olive oil
1 teaspoon salt or tamari (or to taste)
1 teaspoon chopped green onion
1 tablespoon raw agave nectar or honey
1 teaspoon dried mustard
1 teaspoon paprika
½ teaspoon thyme
2 garlic cloves
---
2 teaspoons dried dill (or 2 tablespoons fresh)

Process all ingredients except dill in the OMNI blender using the 60 second cycle, or until smooth and creamy.

Tomato Basil Dressing

I love love tomato-based dressings and whip them up all the time. Of all those I've made, this is one of our favorites.

3 medium tomatoes, roughly chopped
½ cup cold pressed olive oil
⅓ cup tomato juice or water
3 tablespoons fresh parsley
2 tablespoons lemon juice
2 tablespoons apple cider vinegar
1 tablespoon dried basil (or ½ cup fresh)
2 teaspoons raw agave nectar or honey
¾ teaspoon salt
¼ teaspoon pepper
1 garlic clove
1 green onion, roughly chopped

Process all ingredients in the OMNI blender using the 60 second cycle, or until smooth and creamy.

Herbed Avocado Spread

Spreads & Nut Cheezes

𝒥n spite of the fact that spreads and nut cheezes are usually considered supplementary to the main course, many of the recipes in this section often occupy a prime spot on our raw table. So versatile, they can be enjoyed with veggie sticks, on crackers, breads and even nori sheets. For a makeshift wrap, you can simply spread two or three spoonfuls on lettuce or collard leaves and top with veggie strips and sprouts. Regardless of how you choose to serve the following creations, I promise they won't fail to seduce your taste buds.

Cheddar Cheeze Spread or Dip

This is such a scrumptious cheezy recipe! Enjoy on your favorite crackers/breads, zucchini pasta, pizza or simply with veggie sticks!

1 cup roughly chopped red or orange bell peppers (I like to use both for a milder color.)
¾ cup almonds or cashews, soaked for 8 hours
¼ cup water
2 - 3 tablespoons rolled oats
2 tablespoons nutritional yeast
2 tablespoons lemon juice
2 tablespoons raw tahini
2 teaspoons onion powder
1 teaspoon garlic powder or 1 garlic clove
1 teaspoon salt

Process all ingredients except dill in the OMNI blender using the 60 second cycle, or until smooth and creamy.

Add more water or oats and blend again until desired consistency is reached.

Herbed Avocado Spread

This is a super simple spread with a lovely herb flavor.

1 cup zucchini, peeled and roughly cubed
2 small avocados
2 tablespoons tamari
2 tablespoons cold pressed olive oil
1 tablespoon + 1 teaspoon lemon juice
2 teaspoons dried tarragon
2 teaspoons finely minced fresh thyme or ½ teaspoon dried
1 teaspoon onion powder
Salt, to taste
Dash cayenne

Process all ingredients in the OMNI blender using the 35 second cycle. Scrape the sides down with a spatula then process for another 35 seconds.

Note: You will need to use the tamper in order to keep the mixture moving.

Nacho Cheeze

This is another awesome cheeze, but with a slight bite, and is an ideal component of a Mexican feast such as the Tostada on page 64. It also makes amazing Kale Chips! (See instructions on page 63.)

1 ½ cups cashews, soaked for at least 1 hour
1 ¼ cups roughly chopped red and yellow bell peppers
½ cup water
½ cup roughly chopped carrot (or 1 medium)
2 large garlic cloves
3 tablespoons lime juice
2 tablespoons nutritional yeast
2 teaspoons fajita seasoning
1 ½ teaspoons salt
½ teaspoon Penzey's Spice's North West Fire seasoning or ¼ teaspoon chipotle or cayenne powder

Process all ingredients except dill in the OMNI blender using the 60 second cycle, or until smooth and creamy.

Simple Cream Cheeze

1 ½ cups cashews, soaked for at least 1 hour
½ cup water
1 tablespoon lemon juice
1 ½ teaspoons salt, or to taste

Process all ingredients except dill in the OMNI blender using the 60 second cycle, or until smooth and creamy.

Creamy Spinach Spread

1 recipe Simple Cream Cheeze
3 cups spinach
1 or 2 garlic cloves, to taste
Salt, to taste

1. Pulse-chop the spinach in a food processor until finely minced. (You don't want a green mush though!

2. Gently fold the spinach, garlic and salt into the Simple Cream Cheeze mixture.

Basic Cultured Cashew or Macadamia Cheeze

I had a brief stint with fermented seed and nut cheezes early on my raw journey, using mostly sunflower seeds and almonds. Neither Don nor I were really impressed at the time, so I quickly forgot about it.

My interest was later rekindled when someone posted Chad Sarno's Cashew Cheese Au Poivre on Raw Freedom Community. I was still a little hesitant, remembering my failed experiments, but curiosity got the better of me after reading how delicious it was. I decided to take the plunge and give raw nut cheeze another chance. I don't know what I did wrong before, or perhaps it was just a matter of what type of nuts/seeds I used, but Cashew/Macadamia Cheeze is a whole different story. The result is simply unbelievable; so similar to the 'real thing' in look, texture and even flavor! I like working with both of the nuts. I find that macadamias give a slightly whiter and firmer cheeze.

What you'll need:

- **3 cups cashews, soaked 12 hours or macadamias, soaked 4 hours**
- **1 - 1 ⅓ cups water**
- **4 capsules probiotics**

1. Process ingredients in the OMNI blender using the 35 second cycle. Scrape down the sides with a spatula then process for another 35 seconds. You may need to use the tamper in order to keep the mixture moving in the container.

2. Line a strainer with a double thickness of cheesecloth and place over a bowl.

3. Transfer the mixture to the cheesecloth-lined strainer and cover with a plate. Place a weight on top (I use a 2-quart mason jar filled with water and a book or two) so as to gently press some of the liquid out. If the cheeze pushes through the cloth/strainer, then either the weight is too heavy or the holes of the strainer are too big.

4. Leave in a warm place to culture for 36 to 48 hours. The culturing time will depend on how warm your house is and how 'ripe' you like your cheeze.

5. Once your Basic Cashew or Macadamia Cheeze is ready, you can then season it according to one of the recipes in this book or with whatever flavors you want, such as garlic and chives, sun dried tomatoes and olives, fresh basil, rosemary and thyme, or jalapeño pepper. So many variations to play with!

Notes:

~ For best results in terms of texture, it is key to use as little liquid as possible. For macadamia nuts I find that I need more water (about 1 ⅓ cups) in order to obtain a creamy cheeze.

~ You could substitute the probiotics with miso; the idea is to give the culture a kick-start.

~ I once forgot to soak cashews ahead of time and simply ground them up finely in the OMNI first. The mixture didn't blend as easily as with soaked cashews, so I ended up using more liquid than in the original recipe.

~ If you feel this recipe yields more cheeze than you can eat in a week, simply freeze a portion of it in an airtight container, before or after it's been seasoned.

Basil & Garlic Cheeze

My discovery of cultured cashew and macadamia cheezes has been a true revelation for me. They taste and look exactly like traditional cream cheese, and they never fail to impress whomever I serve them to. Try one of the following variations or you can come up with your own combination!

1 cup Basic Cashew Cheeze (recipe on page 52)
1 tablespoon packed fresh basil, chopped
1 generous teaspoon minced garlic
1 teaspoon minced chives
1 teaspoon nutritional yeast
1 teaspoon onion powder
½ teaspoon salt
¼ teaspoon lemon juice

Dried basil and garlic powder for the crust

1. Place all the ingredients except for the dried basil and garlic powder in a bowl. Stir until well combined. Taste and adjust the salt, as needed.

2. Press the mixture firmly into a small container or bowl lined with plastic film. Sprinkle the dried basil and garlic powder on top. Chill for at least 12 hours to allow flavors to mingle and the Cheeze to firm up.

3. When firm, de-mold, turn over and transfer Cheeze onto a plate. Sprinkle more dried herbs on top and sides.

4. Store in the refrigerator in an airtight container for up to one week.

Variation: You can enjoy this Cheeze 'cream cheese style' by transferring the mixture directly into a container and using it as a spread.

Herb & Green Onion Cheeze

This is one of the very first cheeze variations that I have experimented with. Delish!

1 cup Basic Cashew Cheeze (recipe on page 52)
1 ½ teaspoons minced green onion
1 teaspoon chopped fresh basil (or ½ teaspoon dried)
1 teaspoon chopped fresh thyme (or ½ teaspoon dried)
1 teaspoon nutritional yeast
½ teaspoon salt
¼ teaspoon lemon juice

Dried basil and thyme for the crust

1. Place all the ingredients except dried basil and thyme for the crust in a bowl. Stir until well combined. Taste and adjust salt, as needed.

2. Press the mixture firmly into a small container or bowl lined with plastic film. Sprinkle the dried herbs on top. Chill for at least 12 hours to allow flavors to blend and the Cheeze to firm up.

3. Proceed as for Basil & Garlic Cheeze on page 53.

Garlic & Dill Cheeze

As I love fresh dill, this is one of my favorite cheezes.

1 cup Basic Cashew Cheeze (recipe on page 52)
1 tablespoon minced fresh dill
1 generous teaspoon minced garlic
1 teaspoon minced chives
1 teaspoon nutritional yeast
1 teaspoon onion powder
½ teaspoon salt
¼ teaspoon lemon juice

Finely ground almonds, dried dill and garlic powder for the crust (optional)

1. Place all the ingredients except ground almonds, dried dill and garlic powder for the crust in a bowl. Stir until well combined. Taste and adjust the salt, as needed.

2. Press the mixture firmly into a small container or bowl lined with plastic film. Sprinkle the ground almonds, dried dill and garlic powder on top. Chill for at least 12 hours to allow flavors to mingle and the Cheeze to firm up.

3. Proceed as for Basil & Garlic Cheeze on page 53.

Herbed Almonnaise

This mayonnaise is made with almonds and is fantastic on bread or crackers with a slice of tomato and some fresh sprouts, as a dip for veggies, or even thinned out as a dressing.

½ cup almonds, finely ground
½ cup cold water (put 2 ice cubes in the water)
1 ½ teaspoons raw honey or agave nectar
1 teaspoon nutritional yeast
1 teaspoon unsalted herbal seasoning
¾ teaspoon salt
⅛ teaspoon mustard powder
⅛ teaspoon ground black pepper
2 cloves garlic
---
1 cup cold pressed olive oil
3 tablespoons lemon juice
½ teaspoon apple cider vinegar

1. Process the first 9 ingredients in the OMNI blender using the 60 second cycle, or until smooth.

2. With the blender on low, pour the oil in a thin stream through the top's small opening.

3. With the blender still running, add lemon juice and apple cider vinegar. Continue to blend on low for a few more seconds. For a plain almonnaise, stop here.

For a Herbed Almonnaise: Add and blend only to incorporate:
2 teaspoons dried basil
2 teaspoons dried tarragon
1 teaspoon dried dill
1 small green onion, minced

Refrigerate in an airtight container. It will keep for about 10 days.

Notes:

~ The purpose of the ice cubes is to thicken the mixture. If the almonnaise seems runny after adding the oil, add another ice cube or two to help thicken it up again. Bear in mind that it will also get firmer when refrigerated.

~ You can make your own herb blend by using your favorite dried or fresh herbs.

Sauces & Savory Dishes

Sauces are so versatile! They have the fantastic ability to turn the blandest dish into an exciting and exotic affair! In traditional cuisine however, they are usually laden with cooked fats, dairy and flour. The good news is that infinitely healthier succulent alternatives can be prepared in no time with the help of a blender! Enjoy the delicious sauces and condiments in this section as dips, marinades, spreads and on top of vegetable pasta or your favorite grain.

For a warm sauce, simply heat up gently on a medium stove while stirring constantly to make sure that the precious enzymes stay alive.

Cheezy Cannellonis

These are so simple to make! Fill, roll, top with tomato sauce and voila!

'PASTA'
1 medium zucchini, peeled

First, cut your zucchini lengthwise into 2 halves. Then slice thin long strips using a mandoline or V-slicer. Set aside.

CREAMY SPINACH SPREAD
Recipe on page 51

TOMATO SAUCE
1 cup sun-dried tomatoes, soaked
2 or 3 medium tomatoes, roughly chopped
2 tablespoons cold pressed olive oil
2 small soft dates, soaked for a few minutes (or 1 Medjhool)
1 teaspoon salt
1 clove garlic or more, to taste
Fresh or dried herbs, to taste

Drain the sun-dried tomatoes well by giving them a gentle squeeze.

Process all ingredients in the OMNI blender using the 60 second cycle. Adjust seasonings to taste.

ASSEMBLY
1. Place 3 or 4 (depending on the size) strips of zucchini side by side, slightly overlapping. You want to create a squarish shape.

2. Place a couple of tablespoons of Creamy Spinach Spread at one end of the zucchini strips and gently roll up.

3. Repeat until all the zucchini strips and filling are used up.

4. Serve topped with Tomato Sauce.

Variation: For bite-size cannellonis, use a single strip of zucchini at a time.

Note: You might want to spoon on the tomato sauce at the last minute, as it tends to pool up in the plate. An alternative would be to put a little sauce on the plates first, then lay on the cannellonis and serve with more sauce

'Pasta' in Alfredo Sauce

Sooooooo creamy and completely dairy free!

ZUCCHINI PASTA
2 or 3 zucchinis, peeled

Make linguine like pasta with the help of a spiral slicer or veggie peeler. (Although any size would work well too.)

ALFREDO SAUCE
1 cup cashews and/or macadamia nuts, soaked for 1 hour
½ to ¾ cup water (depending on the desired thickness)
3 tablespoons lemon juice
1 teaspoon salt
1 garlic clove

Process all ingredients in the OMNI using the 60 second cycle, or until smooth and creamy.

If desired, serve with marinated mushrooms. (Simply toss mushroom slices in equal parts olive oil and tamari and 1 -2 crushed garlic cloves and allow to marinate for one hour.)

'Peanut' Sauce

In raw food cuisine, raw almond butter and tahini are often combined to simulate the flavor of peanuts. (We also feel they're a much healthier choice!)

3 tablespoons raw almond butter
2 tablespoons raw tahini
2 ½ tablespoons lime juice
1 tablespoon tamari
1 tablespoon raw sesame or coconut oil
1 tablespoon cold pressed olive oil
½ tablespoon grated fresh ginger root
½ teaspoon salt
¼ - ½ teaspoon red pepper flakes
1 ½ Medjhools (or 3 small soft dates)
⅓ - ½ cup water, to taste
2 garlic cloves

Process all ingredients in the OMNI blender using the 60 second cycle, or until smooth and creamy. If necessary, add more water until the desired consistency is reached.

Enjoy as a dip or on top on your favorite veggie or grain pasta.

Ginger Dipping Sauce or Marinade

This Ginger Sauce is fantastic either as a dip for Spring Rolls or as a marinade! We let the vegetables marinate for at least one hour, then serve them on a bed of noodles of our choice, adding extra sauce to taste. This is one of Don's favorite dishes!

1 cup raw sesame or cold pressed olive oil
¼ cup lemon or lime juice
¼ cup tamari
¼ cup grated ginger
1 ½ - 2 teaspoons red pepper flakes
2 Medjhools (or 4 small soft dates)
2 garlic cloves

Process all ingredients in the OMNI using the 60 second cycle, or until smooth and creamy.

Pad Thai Sauce

¼ cup cashews
¼ cup sun-dried tomatoes, soaked for 1 hour
2 tablespoons tamari, or to taste
1 heaping tablespoon raw tahini
1 tablespoon raw almond butter
1 tablespoon lime juice
2 teaspoons curry powder, to taste
½ teaspoon salt, or to taste
1-2 garlic cloves
1 Medjhool (or 2 small soft dates, pitted and soaked for 1 hour)
1 tablespoon grated fresh ginger
½ cup + 2 tablespoons tomato soaking water

Process all ingredients in the OMNI blender using the 60 second cycle, or until smooth.

If necessary, add more water until the desired consistency is reached.

Serve on noodles of your choice. Top with diced red or yellow peppers and marinated Portobellos. Sprinkle with freshly chopped cilantro.

Cauliflower Curry

My love of Indian cuisine goes back to my early twenties when I worked at an East Indian restaurant in England. I'll never forget the wondrous sight of the cook expertly dipping the tip of his large metal spoon into an array of colorful spices while preparing a curry. Flames leapt from the gas stove and the most exquisite aroma would start filling the kitchen. I have tried repeatedly to recreate curries at home, but they always fell ridiculously short of authentic Indian cuisine. One of the exciting culinary discoveries we made while in the US was Penzeys Spices, a company that sells wonderfully fresh and fragrant spices. I was pleasantly surprised by their many curry blends; Balti, Sweet Curry, Tandoori, Vindaloo, Maharajah Style... each so delicate and unique. The following Curry Sauce is undoubtedly the best one to have ever come out of my kitchen, raw or cooked! Absolutely delightful!

One of our favorite ways to serve it is with Marinated Cauliflower.

Yields about 2 cups

CURRY SAUCE
1 cup roughly chopped red bell pepper
¾ cup cashews, soaked for at least 1 hour
⅓ cup roughly chopped carrot
2 tablespoons cold pressed olive oil
2 tablespoons apple cider vinegar
1 tablespoon raw honey or agave nectar
1 tablespoon nutritional yeast

1 tablespoon water
2 teaspoons curry (I use Penzey's Spices' Sweet Curry)
2 garlic cloves (or 1 teaspoon garlic powder)
1 teaspoon cumin
1 teaspoon coriander seeds
1 teaspoon onion powder
1 teaspoon salt
½ teaspoon chili powder
⅛ teaspoon cayenne

Process all ingredients in the OMNI blender using the 60 second cycle, or until smooth and creamy.

Note: If you use a different brand of curry powder, add an extra teaspoon or two of honey or agave nectar.

MARINATED CAULIFLOWER

Cauliflower is one of those veggies we didn't particularly care for in the raw because it develops such a strong pungent flavor as it sits due to oxidation. When I saw that Russell James was marinating it in his Cauliflower Cheese recipe, I thought that I'd at least give it a try, since almost everything I've made of his has been excellent. Low and behold, it really did the trick! The marinating process successfully took away the cauliflower's distasteful edge. This is the technique I used in this recipe.

1 medium head of cauliflower, broken into florets
1 tablespoon lemon juice
1 tablespoon cold pressed olive oil
¾ teaspoon salt
¼ teaspoon turmeric

ASSEMBLY

1. Toss the Marinated Cauliflower with some Curry Sauce. (You may not need to use it all.)

2. Place in the dehydrator at 110ºF for 1 or 2 hours. (optional)

3. Serve on top of a bed of your favorite vegetable rice or grains.

Variation: CURRIED KALE CHIPS

This Curry Sauce also makes the most delicious kale chips!

1. Wash, dry and de-stem 2 large bunches of kale.

2. Break the kale into chip size pieces.

3. Place the kale pieces in a large bowl, pour the Curry Sauce on top and mix thoroughly with your hands.

4. Transfer the coated kale pieces to dehydrator trays covered with non-stick sheets.

5. Dehydrate at 110ºF for 3 hours or until the top feels dry to the touch, then flip the coated kale onto the mesh. Continue dehydrating until fully dry.

6. Store in an airtight container or Ziploc bags in a cool and dry place.

Raw Tostada

Have yourself a fiesta and enjoy this raw vegan version of a Mexican classic!

GUACAMOLE
2 medium avocados, peeled and pitted
2 tablespoons lime or lemon juice
1 tablespoon cumin
1 ½ teaspoons salt
2 garlic cloves, crushed
Cayenne or chipotle powder, to taste
2 tablespoons water
1 cup chopped tomatoes (optional)
½ cup fresh cilantro, chopped

Process all ingredients except tomatoes and cilantro in the OMNI blender using the 35 second cycle. Scrape down the sides with a spatula then process for another 35 seconds. You may need to use the tamper to keep the mixture moving in the container. Transfer to a bowl. Add the chopped cilantro and tomatoes (if using) and mash with a fork.

FRESH TOMATO SALSA
4 medium tomatoes, roughly chopped
½ cup roughly chopped red onion
1 or 2 jalapeno peppers, seeded and roughly chopped
2 tablespoons lime juice
1 teaspoon salt
2 garlic cloves
¼ cup finely chopped fresh cilantro

Process all ingredients except cilantro in the OMNI blender using the pulse button. Transfer to a bowl and fold in the chopped cilantro. Allow to sit for an hour in order for the flavors to blend.

NACHO CHEEZE
Recipe on page 50

CASHEW SOUR CREAM
1 cup cashews or macadamia nuts, soaked for 1 hour
½ cup water
1 tablespoon lemon juice
1 tablespoon apple cider vinegar
½ teaspoon salt

Process all ingredients in the OMNI blender using the 60 second cycle, or until smooth and creamy.

Store in the refrigerator in an airtight container.

ASSEMBLY
Make a bed of your favorite dehydrated or traditional corn chips or tortillas.

Top with a few spoonfuls of Guacamole, followed by Nacho Cheeze.

Cover with slivered lettuce.

Finish off with some Fresh Tomato Salsa and a drizzle of Cashew Sour Cream.

If desired, sprinkle with finely chopped fresh cilantro.

Basil Pesto

This is another popular traditional sauce with a raw vegan twist. Toss the pesto with zucchini made into raw 'pasta' (with the help of a spiralizer or veggie peeler), or simply pour on top of your favorite whole grain pasta.

4 cups fresh basil and spinach, packed (I like to use ½ of each)
¼ cup walnuts
½ teaspoon salt
2 tablespoons cold pressed olive oil
1 tablespoon nutritional yeast
2 teaspoons lemon juice
2 large garlic cloves

Process all ingredients in the OMNI blender using the 60 second cycle, or until smooth.

Desserts

*B*y now, you should have a pretty good sense that the raw food diet is not about sacrifice and austere deprivation. As you have seen, you can make all sorts of incredibly tasty smoothies, super creamy soups, sexy salads and raw gourmet dishes. However for me, desserts are 'creating in the raw' in its most stunning and delectable form. What's more, they have all the scrumptious looks and palatable tastes of the most exquisite traditional desserts... minus the undesirable side effects. Guilt-free decadence? Mmmmmmmm... Now we're talking!

Chocolate Mousse

An avocado based chocolate mousse or pudding is probably one of the first sweet treats one learns to prepare in a raw kitchen. It's unbelievably creamy, full of goodness and the fact that it contains avocado almost always surprises those people new to raw. This is my version of this popular dessert.

2 medium (or 3 small) avocados
½ - ⅔ cup raw honey or agave nectar
¼ cup water
3 tablespoons cacao powder
2 tablespoons carob powder
½ teaspoon pure vanilla extract or liquid vanilla
Pinch of salt

1. Process all ingredients in the OMNI blender using the 60 second cycle, or until smooth and creamy. You may need to use the tamper to keep the mixture moving.

2. Pour the mixture into serving glasses or bowls. Chill for a couple of hours.

3. If desired, serve with fresh berries and Cashew Whipped Cream on page 70.

Variation - *Chocolate Pie:*

1. After blending the rest of the ingredients, add:

¼ cup melted coconut oil or 2 tablespoons melted cacao butter
1 tablespoon lecithin powder

2. Continue blending until completely smooth.

3. Pour over a nut crust of your choice.

4. Chill in the refrigerator or freezer until firm.

Mango Pudding With Vanilla Coconut Custard

Another simple dessert that can be prepared in no time at all. Oh, and utterly delicious too!

Serves 3

PUDDING
3 cups mango, peeled, pitted and roughly chopped
1 large frozen banana
Juice of 1 lime
3 soft dates, pitted and soaked for 1 hour

Process all ingredients in the OMNI blender using the 60 second cycle, or until smooth.

VANILLA COCONUT CUSTARD
1 cup coconut meat
½ cup coconut water
½ cup cashews, soaked for 1 hour
2 ½ tablespoons raw agave nectar or 4 soft dates, pitted and soaked for 1 hour
2 tablespoons melted coconut oil
1 teaspoon pure vanilla extract or liquid vanilla
¼ teaspoon salt

Process all ingredients in the OMNI blender using the 60 second cycle, or until smooth.

ASSEMBLY
Pour some Mango Pudding in a serving bowl and top with Vanilla Coconut Custard.

Cashew Whipped Cream

This is a dairy-free alternative to Whipped Cream that's every bit as scrumptious tasting but minus the negative side effects! Enjoy it on fresh fruits, puddings or whatever desserts for an extra touch of healthy decadence!

Adapted from a recipe by Café Gratitude

1 cup cashews
1 cup + 2 tablespoons coconut milk (recipe on page 27)
3 tablespoons raw honey or agave nectar
1 tablespoon lemon juice
1 tablespoon pure vanilla extract or liquid vanilla
Pinch salt

½ cup melted coconut oil
1 tablespoon lecithin powder

1. Process all ingredients except the melted coconut oil and lecithin in the OMNI blender using the 60 second cycle, or until smooth.

2. Add the coconut oil and lecithin and blend briefly, just to incorporate.

3. Pour into a container and chill in the refrigerator until firm.

Chocolate Sauce

Drizzle on pieces of fruit, ice cream, or whatever sweet treat you like!

½ cup cacao powder
¼ cup carob powder
¼ cup + 2 tablespoons raw agave nectar
¼ cup maple syrup
2 tablespoons pure vanilla extract or liquid vanilla
½ cup melted coconut oil
2 pinches salt

Process all ingredients in the OMNI blender using the 60 second cycle, or until smooth.

Keep refrigerated in airtight container. To liquify it again, simply warm up over a bowl of hot water while stirring.

Persimmon & Coconut Cream Parfait

I find that persimmons have a very subtle flavor that can very easily get lost when combined with other ingredients. This parfait is lovely and light, and is a wonderful way to enjoy this delicate fruit.

Serves 4

SIMPLE PERSIMMON PUDDING
Flesh of 4 very ripe persimmons

Process persimmons in the OMNI blender using the 35 second cycle, or until smooth.

COCONUT CREAM
¼ cup young coconut meat
⅔ cup coconut water
¼ cup + 2 tablespoons cashews, soaked for 1 hour
⅛ - ¼ cup raw honey or agave nectar, to taste
1 teaspoon lucuma (optional)
1 teaspoon vanilla extract
Pinch salt

¼ cup melted coconut oil
2 teaspoons lecithin powder

Process all ingredients except coconut oil and lecithin in the OMNI blender using the 60 second cycle, or until smooth.

Add coconut oil and lecithin and blend briefly, just to incorporate.

Chill to firm up.

TROPICAL CRUMBLE LAYER AND/OR TOPPING (OPTIONAL)
2 tablespoons dried coconut
1 tablespoon gogi berries
1 tablespoon dried mango

Finely grind the coconut, gogi berries and mango in a coffee grinder.

Note: The topping idea came to me when I was almost done assembling the parfaits, but layering some of the mixture between layers would also be visually stunning; it's so colorful and pretty.

ASSEMBLY
In a nice glass, place a couple of spoonfuls of Persimmon Pudding, followed by some Coconut Cream. Alternatively, for a different effect, you could start with the Cream, followed by the pudding.

If desired, sprinkle a layer of Tropical Crumble mixture.

Repeat layers, finishing off with more Tropical Crumble.

Cheesecake with Raspberry Sauce

I probably had traditional cheesecake only twice in my entire life. (I'm not kidding!) All that sugar and dairy... No thanks! What can I say, I was never a big fan of desserts. (I mean, prior to getting into raw!) Because of that, I was initially a little suspicious of raw cheesecake. I kept procrastinating and procrastinating until I could no longer ignore all the hoots and raves about it.

Imagine my surprise (and delight!) when I discovered that while raw cheesecake is sweet, creamy and rich, the resemblance to its infamous twin stops there. It is a perfect example of how the 'living' version of a recipe can surpass the SAD one in every way.

Makes one 7-inch cake

CRUST
1 cup almonds
¼ cup soft dates
⅛ teaspoon pure vanilla extract or liquid vanilla
Pinch salt

Process the ingredients in a food processor until crumbly. The mixture should stick when pressed together between your fingers. If it's too dry, add a little water or some agave if it isn't quite sweet enough (1 teaspoon or so at a time.)

Press into the bottom of a 7-inch springform pan, or into a pie plate.

FILLING
2 cups cashews, soaked for at least 1 hour
½ cup water
½ cup raw honey or agave nectar
2 tablespoons lemon juice
1 ½ teaspoons pure vanilla extract or liquid vanilla

¼ cup + 2 tablespoons melted coconut oil
1 tablespoon lecithin powder

1. Process first five ingredients in the OMNI blender using the 60 second cycle, or until smooth.

2. Add the melted coconut oil and lecithin and blend briefly, just to incorporate.

3. Pour the filling onto the crust. Chill the cake in the refrigerator or freezer for a few hours, or until firm.

~ Add any kind of fresh fruit (berries are particularly great!) to this cheesecake, either inside or layered on the surface.

~ Serve drizzled with a Berry Jam or Sauce.

BERRY JAM OR SAUCE
1 ½ cups fresh or frozen berries such as blueberry, raspberry, strawberry, etc.
1 or 2 tablespoons raw honey or agave nectar
Juice of ½ lemon

For a jam, mix all ingredients by hand, crushing the berries with a fork.

For a sauce, process all ingredients in the OMNI blender using the 35 second cycle or until smooth.

Note: Strain if using raspberries so as to remove the seeds.

Bliss-full Blueberry Cheesecake

This is a decadent and gorgeous cake inspired by Vanessa Sherwood's fantastic White Chocolate-Strawberry Cheesecake. A taste of raw heaven...

Makes one 7" cheesecake

CRUST
½ cup Brazil nuts
¼ cup almonds
¼ cup shredded coconut
1 tablespoon cacao or carob powder
1 teaspoon pure vanilla extract or liquid vanilla
Pinch of salt
2 Medjhool dates
1 teaspoon raw agave nectar

Process the ingredients in a food processor until crumbly. The mixture should stick when pressed together between your fingers. If it's too dry, add a little water or some agave if it isn't quite sweet enough (1 teaspoon or so at a time.) Press into the bottom of a 7-inch springform pan, or into a pie plate.

FILLING

2 cups fresh or frozen blueberries (thawed)
1 cup cashews, finely ground
¼ cup + 2 tablespoons melted coconut oil
2 tablespoons melted cacao butter
¼ cup raw honey or agave nectar
1 tablespoon lemon juice
⅛ teaspoon salt

Process all ingredients in the OMNI blender using the 60 second cycle, or until smooth and creamy. You may need to use the tamper in order for the mixture to keep moving.

Pour the filling over the crust and chill or freeze until ready to serve.

Note: If using frozen blueberries, make sure they are well thawed to avoid the honey turning rock hard while blending.

BLUEBERRY SAUCE

1 cup blueberries, fresh or frozen
Agave nectar to taste

If desired, decorate with Blueberry Sauce or Chocolate Sauce (recipe on page 69) and blueberries.

Dazzling Hazelnut Cream Pie

This is one of my favorite pies; a rich chocolate avocado mousse with a hazelnut touch. To live for!

Makes one 9-inch pie

CRUST
1 cup macadamia nuts
½ cup dried coconut
½ cup hazelnuts
2 teaspoons pure vanilla extract or liquid vanilla
2 pinches salt
4 Medjhool dates

Place the first 5 ingredients in a food processor and process until fine.

Add the dates and process until the dough 'sticks' together when pressed between fingers. If it's too dry, add a little water or agave if it isn't quite sweet enough (1 teaspoon or so at a time.) Press in the bottom of a 9-inch pie crust and set aside.

FILLING
3 small or 2 medium avocados
¾ cup hazelnut milk (recipe on page 27)
¼ cup water
¼ cup soft dates
¼ cup + 2 tablespoons raw agave nectar
2 tablespoons maple syrup

⅓ cup + 1 tablespoon cacao powder
2 teaspoons pure vanilla extract or liquid vanilla
1 teaspoon pure almond extract
2 teaspoons coffee substitute powder such as Inka
¼ teaspoon salt

½ cup melted coconut oil
2 tablespoons lecithin powder

1. Process all ingredients except last two in the OMNI blender using the 60 second cycle, or until smooth. You may need to use the tamper in order for the mixture to keep moving.

2. Add the melted coconut oil and lecithin and blend briefly, just to incorporate.

3. Pour the filling over the crust and place in the refrigerator or freezer to set.

4. If desired, decorate with cacao powder passed through a sieve and hazelnuts.

Note: If you wish, you could replace the almond extract and coffee substitute powder called for in the filling recipe with 1 tablespoon hazelnut extract.

Vanilla Ice Cream

The last addition to our raw kitchen has been an ice cream maker. As they are relatively inexpensive (we paid about $70 for a 'top of the line' Cuisinart Indulgence 2-quarts) I figured it would be a good investment. We can now treat ourselves to heavenly homemade raw vegan ice creams that are also super simple to whip up. The secret to avoid the ice cream being 'crystally' rather than smooth and creamy is to ensure that your mixture has a high enough fat content (usually in the form of nuts, nut milk, young coconut meat or coconut oil). Here is a delicious vanilla ice cream base that can be easily modified to include your favorite flavors.

Yields approximately one quart

1 ½ cups cashews, soaked for 4 hours
1 cup water
¾ cup young coconut meat
½ cup + 1 tablespoon raw agave nectar
1 ½ tablespoons pure vanilla extract or liquid vanilla
¼ cup melted coconut oil
¼ teaspoon salt

1. Process all ingredients in the OMNI blender using the 60 second cycle, or until smooth and creamy.

2. Chill the mixture in the refrigerator or freezer, then process through an ice cream maker according to the manufacturer's instructions. Alternatively, freeze the mixture in ice cube trays and process briefly through the OMNI blender to soften up.

Chocolate Ice Cream

Our friend Livina declared this to be THE best chocolate ice cream she has ever tasted!

Yields approximately one quart

1 ½ cups cashews, soaked for 4 hours
1 cup water
¾ cup young coconut meat
½ cup + 3 tablespoons raw agave nectar
½ cup cacao powder
3 tablespoons maple syrup
2 tablespoons pure vanilla extract or liquid vanilla
¼ cup melted coconut oil
¼ teaspoon salt

Proceed as for Vanilla Ice Cream recipe on page 77.

Banana Vanilla Chocolate Sundae

Although I was never a big fan of desserts, as a child ice cream sundaes used to be one of the few sweet treats I really liked. Once again, raw allows me to enjoy an old favorite without having to worry about a sugar rush or getting a runny nose from the dairy.

Serves 2

For this recipe you will need:
- **Vanilla and Chocolate Ice Cream(s) on pages 77 and 78**
- **1 ripe banana, sliced**
- **Chocolate Sauce (recipe on page 69)**
- **Nuts of your choice, such as pecans and walnuts, roughly chopped**

1. Place banana slices in a bowl.

2. Add a couple of scoops of each ice cream.

3. Drizzle with Chocolate Sauce and top with nut pieces.

4. Close your eyes and enjoy with candor!

Index

Resources

Carmella's Websites

www.thesunnyrawkitchen.blogspot.com

www.rawfreedomcommunity.info/forum

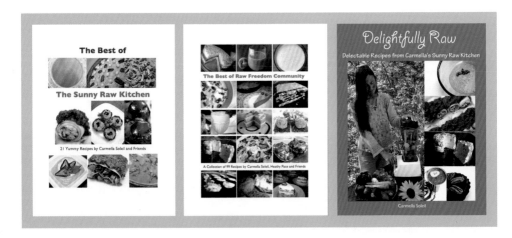

Carmella's Recipe Books (available on **www.thesunnyrawkitchen.blogspot.com**)

The Best of The Sunny Raw Kitchen

The Best of Raw Freedom Community

Delightfully Raw

Omniblend V Blender

To find out more about the Omniblend V blender, please visit The Sunny Raw Kitchen at **www.thesunnyrawkitchen.blogspot.com**